The World Beneath the Waves

written by Catherine Allison

illustrated by Chris Brown and Martin Fish

Contents

Introduction

Oceans cover about three quarters of the Earth's surface. In places they are even deeper than Mount Everest is high.

The saltwater world of the oceans is home to an amazing range of plants and animals. But huge areas of the oceans and their wildlife are as yet unexplored.

The Earth has five oceans. In order of size they are: the Pacific, the Atlantic and the Indian Oceans, the Antarctic or Southern Ocean and the Arctic Ocean. The Pacific is about thirteen times larger than the Arctic Ocean.

In every ocean, from the shallowest to the deepest waters, there is life.

Arctic Ocean

Tropic of Cancer

Atlantic Ocean

Equator

Tropic of Capricorn

Indian Ocean

Pacific Ocean

Antarctic Ocean

How does the wildlife differ from ocean to ocean and from the shallows to the depths? How do sea creatures and plants fit into their unique environment?

The ocean supermarket

What do ocean creatures and plants eat?

Each ocean is like a huge supermarket, providing live food for all its inhabitants. The biggest creatures feed on smaller ones, and they in turn feed on even smaller creatures. Microscopic organisms called **plankton** are the smallest creatures in this **food chain**.

A typical food chain from the Pacific Ocean.

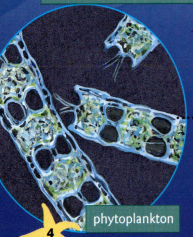

phytoplankton

zooplankton

herring

At the root of every ocean food chain are plants, which range from large seaweeds to tiny algae called phytoplankton.

Plants make their own food using sunlight. As sunlight cannot penetrate water more than about 200 metres deep, plants have to live near the ocean surface.

Plants also need **nutrients** like minerals which they get from river water flowing into the sea and from rainfall.

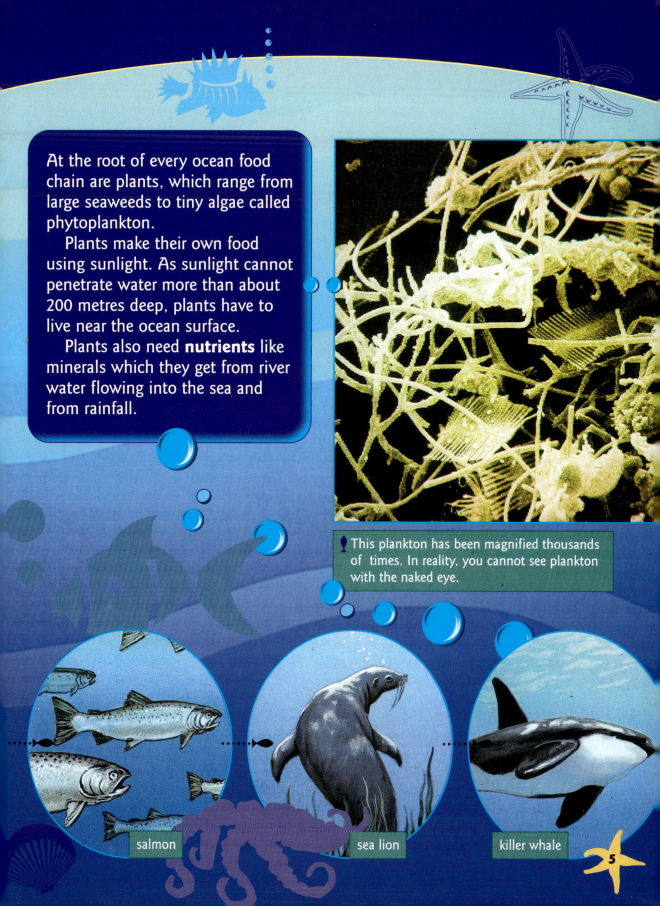

This plankton has been magnified thousands of times. In reality, you cannot see plankton with the naked eye.

salmon

sea lion

killer whale

The ocean home

What sort of environment is home to the ocean creatures? **?**

Some ocean creatures need to live in waters of a particular temperature. Corals, for instance, can live only in warm waters (between 20 and 35 °C). Other creatures can survive in waters of different temperatures at different times in their lives. Grey whales, for example, feed on shrimp-like creatures in the cold Arctic waters but swim thousands of kilometres south to the warm waters off Mexico to breed.

Chukchi Sea

Siberia

Bering Sea

Alaska

Canada

Pacific Ocean

USA

Mexico

➡ Grey whale migration route

Tropic of Cancer

Grey whale and calf migrating

6

Some oceans are more salty than others. Many marine animals can survive only where the salt levels are right for them.

The Atlantic salmon is one of the few creatures able to adapt to either salt sea water or fresh river water. When it is time to breed, it swims from the open sea, where it lives as an adult fish, back to the freshwater river where it was born.

In order to do this, salmon have to change their bodies to cope with the different levels of salt. Some scientists believe that this change is so damaging that they can make the journey only once in a lifetime. Overcome by the change, the Atlantic salmon **spawns** and then dies.

Normal sea water is about one thirtieth dissolved salt, but the Dead Sea, between Israel and Jordan, is almost one third dissolved salt. Very few living things can survive this level of **salinity**, and this is how the Dead Sea got its name.

Salt formations in the Dead Sea

7

As the water gets deeper, it becomes darker and colder, and this dictates which types of marine creatures can live there.

Sharks and dolphins come to feed on the fish.

Nutrients like minerals pour into the sea from the land.

Plant life

Mid-oceanic ridge

A line of underwater mountains, produced by eruptions of molten rock from deep within the Earth.

Continental shelf

This shelf of rock around each continent is covered by shallow sunlit water up to 200 metres deep. This part of the ocean is most rich in marine life. Ninety per cent of the fish caught for people to eat are found in these waters.

Continental slope

The edge of the shelf which slopes steeply into the ocean depths.

Abyssal plain

The deep sea floor, one of the flattest places on Earth, is covered in a thick layer of **sediment** called ooze.

Deep sea trenches

Cracks in the ocean floor, some of which are deeper than the highest mountains on land.

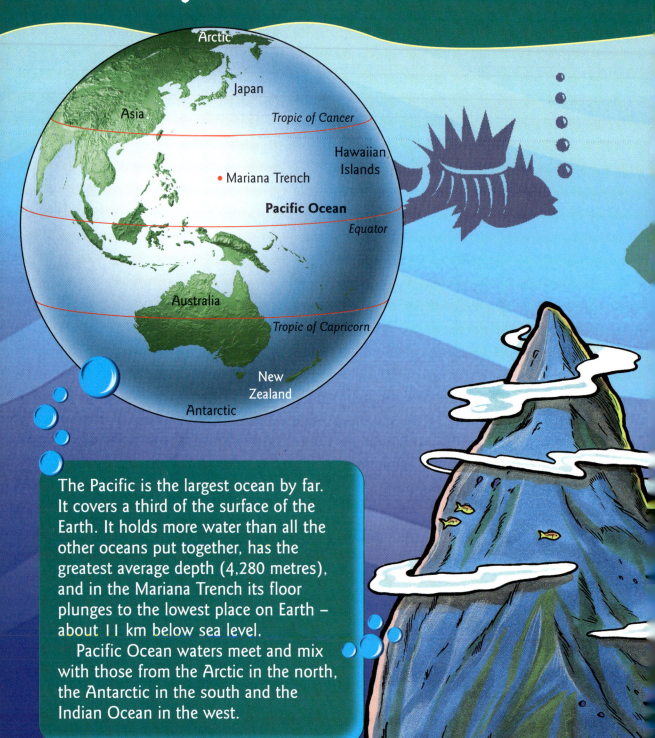

Arctic

Japan

Asia

Tropic of Cancer

Hawaiian Islands

• Mariana Trench

Pacific Ocean

Equator

Australia

Tropic of Capricorn

New Zealand

Antarctic

The Pacific is the largest ocean by far. It covers a third of the surface of the Earth. It holds more water than all the other oceans put together, has the greatest average depth (4,280 metres), and in the Mariana Trench its floor plunges to the lowest place on Earth – about 11 km below sea level.

Pacific Ocean waters meet and mix with those from the Arctic in the north, the Antarctic in the south and the Indian Ocean in the west.

If Mount Everest was placed at the bottom of the Mariana Trench, there would still be over 1.5 km of water above it!

A huge number of plants and animals live in the Pacific Ocean. On the rocky, cold-water coasts of North and South America, there are forests of giant kelp, a type of seaweed which grows to about thirty metres long. There are also large populations of plankton, and fish like herring, sardine and anchovy.

Giant kelp forest

In the tropical region, there is yet more life. These warm waters are home to tuna, and blue whales give birth to their calves here.

Tuna fish

The major oceans: the Atlantic

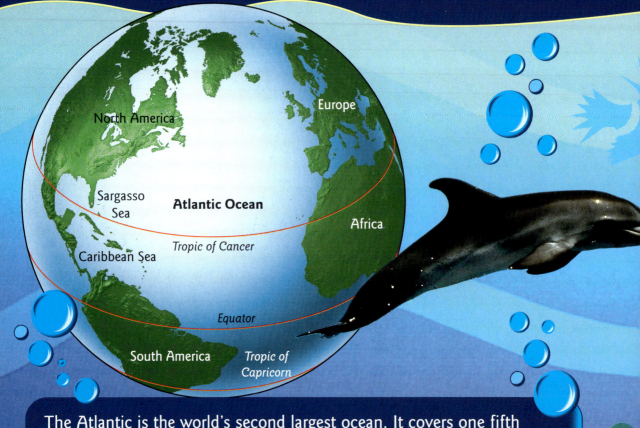

North America

Europe

Sargasso Sea

Atlantic Ocean

Africa

Tropic of Cancer

Caribbean Sea

Equator

South America

Tropic of Capricorn

The Atlantic is the world's second largest ocean. It covers one fifth of the Earth's surface.

Many of the world's great rivers flow into the Atlantic, carrying nutrients from the land. These nutrients and those welling up from the sea bed create a rich **habitat** for plant and animal species, including crabs, **molluscs** and sea turtles.

There is coral in the Caribbean Sea, which is part of the Atlantic; dolphins and harp seals in the north-west Atlantic; and whales in the south Atlantic. The Atlantic Ocean is the most heavily fished in the world, for haddock and cod, lobster, mackerel, hake, tuna and pilchards.

Most of the fish we eat is caught in the Atlantic Ocean.

Spotlight on the freshwater eel

One of the most fascinating creatures to inhabit the Atlantic is the freshwater eel, which **migrates** approximately 3000 km, from its breeding ground in the Sargasso Sea in the west, to its feeding grounds in the freshwater rivers of Europe. The tiny transparent **elvers** are carried eastwards by a warm **current** called the **Gulf Stream** to the European coast, a journey that takes a year and a half. They then swim upstream to the rich feeding grounds, sometimes high up in mountain streams. They will even wriggle along riverbanks to avoid waterfalls, or across fields to reach their goal. After between three and eight years living in fresh water, they have to return to the Sargasso Sea to spawn. Scientists believe that they find their way using the stars and the Earth's magnetic field as aids to navigation.

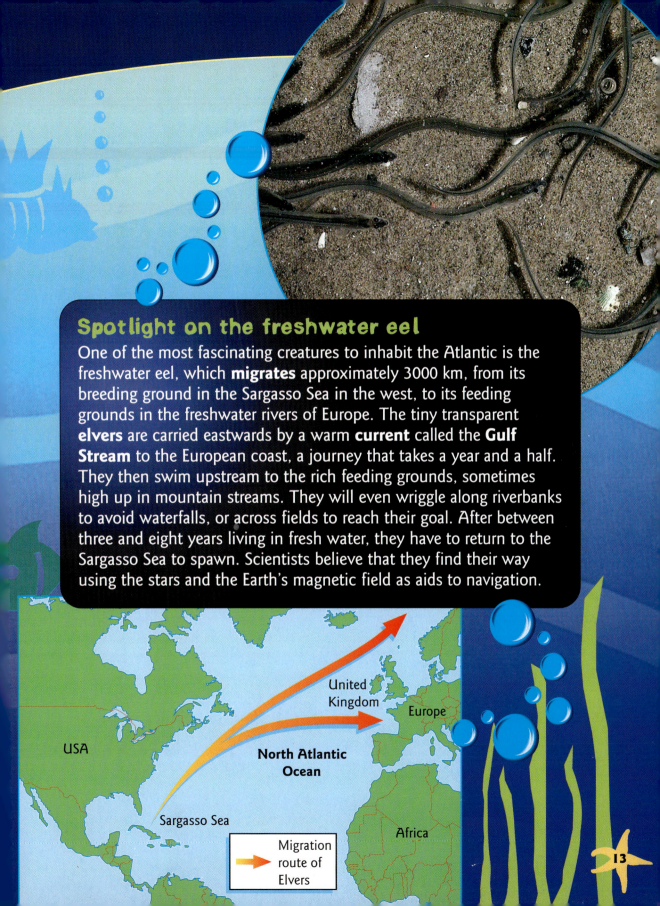

United Kingdom

Europe

USA

North Atlantic Ocean

Sargasso Sea

Africa

Migration route of Elvers

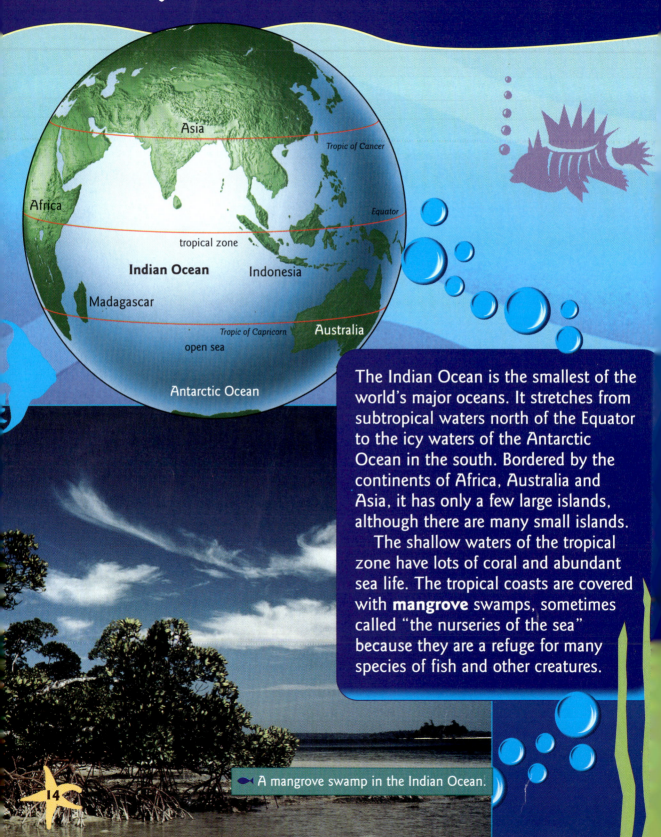

Asia

Tropic of Cancer

Africa

Equator

tropical zone

Indian Ocean Indonesia

Madagascar

Tropic of Capricorn Australia

open sea

Antarctic Ocean

The Indian Ocean is the smallest of the world's major oceans. It stretches from subtropical waters north of the Equator to the icy waters of the Antarctic Ocean in the south. Bordered by the continents of Africa, Australia and Asia, it has only a few large islands, although there are many small islands.

The shallow waters of the tropical zone have lots of coral and abundant sea life. The tropical coasts are covered with **mangrove** swamps, sometimes called "the nurseries of the sea" because they are a refuge for many species of fish and other creatures.

A mangrove swamp in the Indian Ocean.

In the open sea, a hundred species of squid swim in large shoals. Jellyfish include the deadly Portuguese man of war, whose hanging tentacles can grow up to fifty metres in length. Flying fish skim across the surface, supported by their fins and propelled by their tails, and whales, dolphins and seals are often seen.

A shoal of squid

Portuguese man of war

Flying fish

The polar oceans

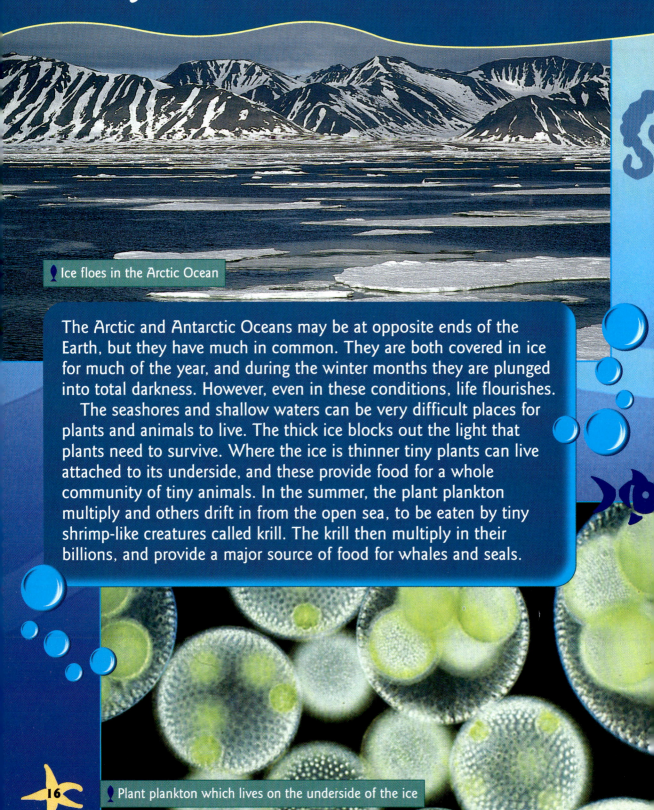

Ice floes in the Arctic Ocean

The Arctic and Antarctic Oceans may be at opposite ends of the Earth, but they have much in common. They are both covered in ice for much of the year, and during the winter months they are plunged into total darkness. However, even in these conditions, life flourishes.

The seashores and shallow waters can be very difficult places for plants and animals to live. The thick ice blocks out the light that plants need to survive. Where the ice is thinner tiny plants can live attached to its underside, and these provide food for a whole community of tiny animals. In the summer, the plant plankton multiply and others drift in from the open sea, to be eaten by tiny shrimp-like creatures called krill. The krill then multiply in their billions, and provide a major source of food for whales and seals.

Plant plankton which lives on the underside of the ice

In deeper waters, there is a huge variety of **invertebrates**, including anemones, prawns and huge sea spiders never seen in warmer waters.

Sea spider

Prawns

Creatures move more slowly in these cold conditions to save energy, and some of them grow to giant size and live many times longer than their relatives in warmer waters. One species of Antarctic limpet can live at least 100 years!

The Antarctic Ocean

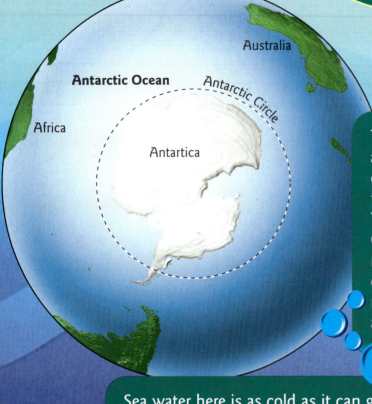

Australia

Antarctic Ocean

Antarctic Circle

Africa

Antartica

The Antarctic Ocean, also known as the Southern Ocean, is a ring of water surrounding the world's fifth largest continent, Antarctica. The Pacific, Atlantic and Indian Oceans all join the Antarctic, mixing warm and cold waters, oxygen and nutrients, and making this one of the most abundant of all the oceans.

Sea water here is as cold as it can get without freezing. In the very long polar winter, there is sunlight for only an hour or two a day, if at all, and sea ice forms on the ocean's surface.

Krill is central to the Antarctic food chain. During the summer months there may be up to six billion **tons** of these tiny reddish crustaceans, each one only as long as a human thumb. Nearly all the ocean's creatures, including whales, fish, seals and penguins, compete to feed on them.

Krill

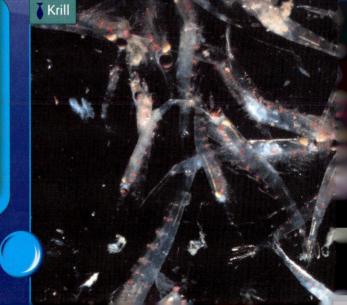

Spotlight on the emperor penguin

Penguins are found only in the southern **hemisphere**. The emperor penguin is the only bird to survive on the Antarctic mainland during the winter. The female lays one egg in autumn and the male then keeps it warm through the height of the Antarctic winter. During this time the male lives on only his body fat, huddling together with other males in huge **colonies** to protect themselves from violent storms and temperatures as low as –70 ˚C. During this time, the female walks up to 160 km from the penguin colony to the sea to feed. After 64 days she reappears as the egg hatches, allowing the male to return to the ocean to seek food.

The Arctic Ocean

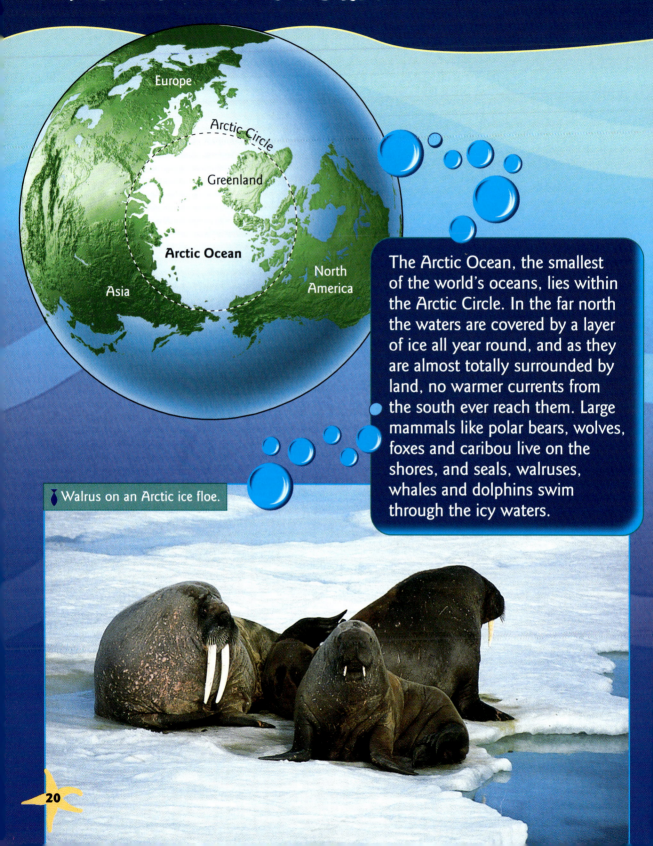

Europe

Arctic Circle

Greenland

Arctic Ocean

North America

Asia

The Arctic Ocean, the smallest of the world's oceans, lies within the Arctic Circle. In the far north the waters are covered by a layer of ice all year round, and as they are almost totally surrounded by land, no warmer currents from the south ever reach them. Large mammals like polar bears, wolves, foxes and caribou live on the shores, and seals, walruses, whales and dolphins swim through the icy waters.

Walrus on an Arctic ice floe.

Spotlight on the ringed seal

The ringed seal protects its pups from predators such as polar bears by giving birth to them in chambers in the ice. The only entrance to each chamber is through the water underneath. Polar bears have a keen sense of smell, which they use to track down their prey, but they cannot smell the pups through the ice. However, the pups must keep very still and quiet inside, or the bears will track them down and use their weight and sharp claws to break through the ice from above.

🐟 Ringed seal pup

The continental shelf

The continental shelf is a sunlit zone which allows a wide variety of plants to grow in the shallow waters. For this reason, it is also rich in fish, reptile and mammal life, as the food supply is so abundant.

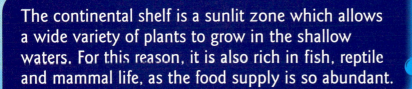
The Great Barrier Reef is 2,000 km long.

Spotlight on coral reefs

In the western Pacific, there are hundreds of islands, and many are surrounded by coral reefs. A single reef can be home to up to 200 kinds of coral, 1500 species of fish, as well as plants, **crustaceans**, and reptiles such as turtles. A coral reef is one of the richest communities of sea life anywhere in the oceans, and the Great Barrier Reef, off north-east Australia, is the world's largest.

With such abundant life the reefs also attract lots of predators, and many reef-dwelling creatures have had to develop clever ways to protect themselves.

Coral may look like rock, but it is made by creatures called polyps. Polyps have soft bodies and mouths ringed by stinging tentacles and they live inside the hard coral. They catch food in their tentacles as it swims past. The coral's bright colours come from algae which live inside the polyps' bodies.

Anemone – a **carnivorous** animal with poisonous tentacles which are used to catch food. Clownfish live amongst its tentacles, and are protected from the poison by a covering of **mucus**.

Stonefish – these fish have poisonous spines in their dorsal fins, and are perfectly camouflaged against the coral surface. Their poison causes humans terrible pain, swelling and breathing difficulties and has been known to kill divers.

Giant clams – also known as killer clams, can reach a weight of 250 kg. A diver who puts a foot in the open shell by mistake could be held underwater and drowned.

The open sea

How have animals adapted to the unprotected environment of the open sea? **?**

Away from the coasts, the ocean waters have fewer nutrients, so plankton and plant life are much more difficult to find. Fish and other creatures living in the open sea need to be able to track down the scarce food, and to protect themselves from being caught or eaten. There are few places to hide.

Predators like sharks are streamlined to swim very fast, and they travel huge distances very quickly. They can sense even tiny electric currents, like a fish's heartbeat, over several kilometres, which helps them to track down food in the vast oceans. They can also detect a single drop of blood in 25 million drops of seawater, so an injured creature is unlikely to escape their jaws.

Smaller fish are often dark on their backs and silver underneath which makes them more difficult to see.

Jellyfish, which cannot move fast, have transparent bodies so that their predators cannot see them easily.

Herrings swim closely together in huge shoals, seventy-five metres across, making it difficult for any one fish to be picked out by an attacker.

The deep ocean

How do animals survive in the dark depths of the ocean? **?**

Between the depths of 200 and 1000 metres, the ocean is cold and dark. Some creatures, like giant squids, swim up to the shallows at night to catch food. Others rely on the remains of dead plants and animals floating down to them from the waters above.

Giant squid

Flashlight fish have bacteria in pouches underneath their eyes, and can turn the light on and off by covering and uncovering them with flaps of skin. Their light can be seen at a distance of thirty metres.

The gulper eel has jaws that stretch almost a quarter of its length, so that it is able to swallow prey much bigger than itself. This means that it can take advantage of any meal it finds.

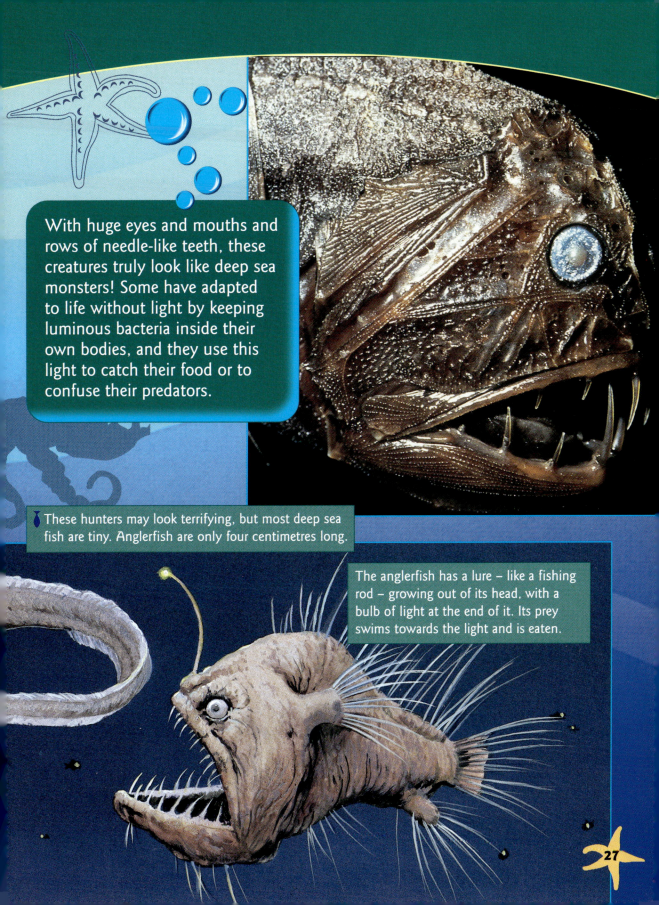

With huge eyes and mouths and rows of needle-like teeth, these creatures truly look like deep sea monsters! Some have adapted to life without light by keeping luminous bacteria inside their own bodies, and they use this light to catch their food or to confuse their predators.

These hunters may look terrifying, but most deep sea fish are tiny. Anglerfish are only four centimetres long.

The anglerfish has a lure – like a fishing rod – growing out of its head, with a bulb of light at the end of it. Its prey swims towards the light and is eaten.

The ocean floor

Are the ocean's floor creatures a clue to life on other planets?

Ninety per cent of ocean waters are deeper than 1000 metres below sea level. Such deep water is totally dark here and very cold. Few creatures can survive these conditions, and those that do must catch and eat what food there is, no matter the size. On the ocean floor live creatures that are like nothing anywhere else on the planet.

Among the creatures living here are tripod fish, which stand on long fins to lift them above the ocean floor, and wait to ambush prey drifting by in the currents.

Here giant sea spiders, whose legs have a span of sixty centimetres, feed by sucking the juices out of soft-bodied crustaceans and worms.

And around the mid-oceanic ridges, where boiling **magma** erupts from deep inside the Earth, scientists have discovered hot mineral springs. Giant tube worms and huge clams and mussels use the minerals to make their food while surviving temperatures of up to 400°C.

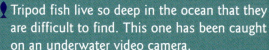
Tripod fish live so deep in the ocean that they are difficult to find. This one has been caught on an underwater video camera.

Mineral springs, or "black smokers", spew out minerals at a temperature of 380 ˚C. Their chimneys can be up to 10 metres tall.

Tube worms, some as long as 1.5 metres, crowd around the hot springs.

Fish called Eelpouts eat the tube worms.

These creatures of the ocean floor are the only ones known on Earth that do not need sunlight to survive, and this discovery has led scientists to think that there could be life forms on other planets using chemicals as a source of energy instead of light.

The wonders of the oceans

The Earth is sometimes called "the blue planet", because so much of its surface is covered by ocean. The animals and plants seen in this book are only a tiny number of the thousands to be found in these waters. It is likely that there are thousands more as yet undiscovered in the oceans' unexplored depths.

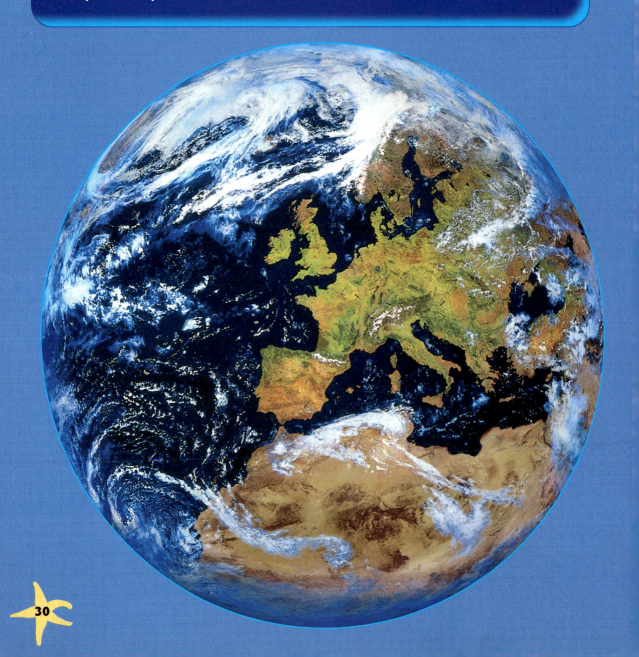

Glossary

carnivorous meat-eating

colony a group of animals or birds

crustacean a shellfish

current the movement of water in a particular direction

elvers young eels

food chain a series of organisms each dependent on the next as a source of food

Gulf Stream an ocean current that carries warm water from the Caribbean Sea up the east coast of the USA to the west coast of northern Europe

habitat natural environment for wildlife

hemisphere half of the globe

invertebrate a soft-bodied creature

magma the fluid material under the Earth's crust

mangroves trees that grow in sea water; their tangled roots are a refuge for marine creatures

migrate to move seasonally to a different region

mollusc a soft-bodied animal, sometimes with an outer shell – oysters and squid are both molluscs

mucus gummy substance

nutrients substances providing nourishment

plankton microscopic plant and animal organisms found in oceans

salinity the amount of salt in the water

sediment matter deposited on the ocean floor

spawn to lay eggs

ton 1000 kilograms

tropics the region between the tropics of Cancer and Capricorn to the north and south of the Equator

Index